SURVIVAL SKILLS HANDBOOK

DESERT

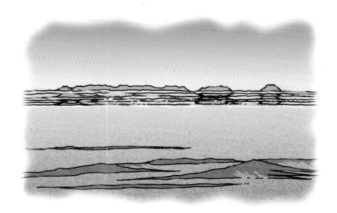

Bear Grylls

This survival handbook has been specially put together to help young adventurers just like you to stay safe in the wild. Adventuring in the desert can be exciting and very fun, but like all environments it presents its own dangers. It is important to be aware of the risks and hazards, and know how to handle yourself in every situation. The desert can be an unforgiving place, so it is vital you are properly prepared before embarking on any adventure. But then, just go for it!

Bear.

CONTENTS

WHAT IS A DESERT?

Almost one third of the world's surface is desert. Most people think of deserts as hot places with little shade, but temperatures vary widely, with extreme cold and high winds at night. Living conditions can be extremely difficult. There is occasional rainfall in the desert but it is only ever a tiny amount, with some places not receiving any at all.

Dry areas
Some deserts have years without rainfall, then a period of heavy rain and flooding.

Polar deserts
Large parts of the polar regions are considered deserts as there is little rainfall.

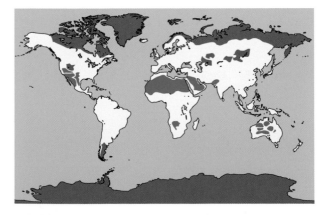

Polar desert
Hot desert

HOW IS A DESERT FORMED?

Deserts are formed by the natural weathering of rocks. Rocks are heated in the daytime and cooled rapidly again at night. This process weakens the rocks and over time causes them to break up into smaller pieces, making sand.

Effects of rain

Rainfall in deserts is usually very low, but occasionally there are sudden, heavy downpours that can cause flooding. These flash floods falling on hot rocks can make them shatter. The wind then picks up the small pieces of rock, sand, and dust and bashes them against other rocks. Over time, rocks are worn away and reduced to sand.

Desert pavements

A desert pavement is a patch of desert ground made up of rocks and stones. This is created when the wind blows away the fine dust and sand covering the rocks.

BEAR SAYS

Most people think of hot and sandy environments when they think of deserts, but this isn't always the case. Antarctica is technically a desert, despite its thick layer of ice, because it has such low rainfall.

RAINFALL EXPLAINED

A desert is any land area that receives less than 250 mm of rainfall per year. One of the driest places on Earth is the Atacama Desert. The lack of rainfall makes it difficult for most plants and animals to survive.

Measuring rainfall

Rainfall is measured using a rain gauge – usually by a meteorologist. The instrument is left outside for a set amount of time, it might be a day, a week, or a year. Then the meteorologist can say how much rain has fallen per year by reading off the scale. This wouldn't work in a rainy climate as the gauge would overflow. Rainfall might have to be measured each hour in some places.

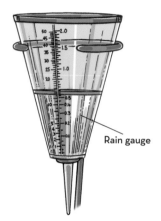

Rain gauge

Living in the desert

This graph shows that the temperature is hottest when the desert has the least amount of rainfall.

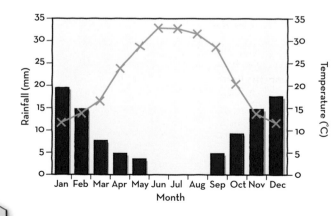

■ Rainfall (mm)

✕ Temperature (°C)

The water cycle

The water cycle is also known as the hydrological cycle. Water on Earth is constantly moving from one stage of the cycle to the next.

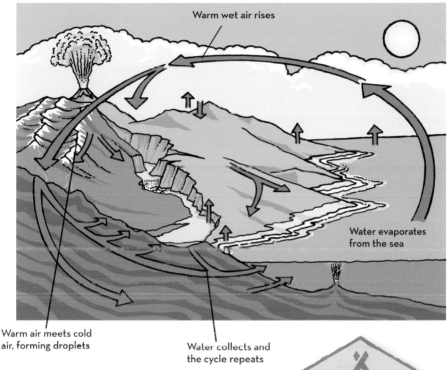

Warm wet air rises

Water evaporates from the sea

Warm air meets cold air, forming droplets

Water collects and the cycle repeats

The cycle

Water moves around the Earth in stages. Heat from the sun evaporates water from the Earth's surface (from lakes, rivers, and oceans). This water vapour rises upward creating warm, wet air. The wet air will travel through the skies until it cools down and condenses into water droplets. When these droplets get too heavy for the air, they begin to fall back to the Earth as rain, sleet, or snow.

BEAR SAYS

Surprisingly, more people die from drowning in flash floods in deserts each year than they do from thirst.

Why doesn't it rain much in the desert?
There are three main reasons why desert rainfall is low.

1. Some deserts are ringed by mountains. These mountains force the winds to cool and the rain to fall before the clouds reach the desert. The Atacama Desert is in a rainshadow between the Andes and the Chilean Coastal Range, meaning it is surrounded by mountain ranges.
2. Some deserts are near the Equator. Air near the Equator is very dry. The air rises and falls again, creating something called high pressure. Air that is moving downward warms up and any water in it becomes a gas so it can't fall as rain.
3. Some desert winds come from the Pacific Ocean. This wind is surprisingly cold but dry as it isn't warm enough to gather moisture from the surface of the ocean.

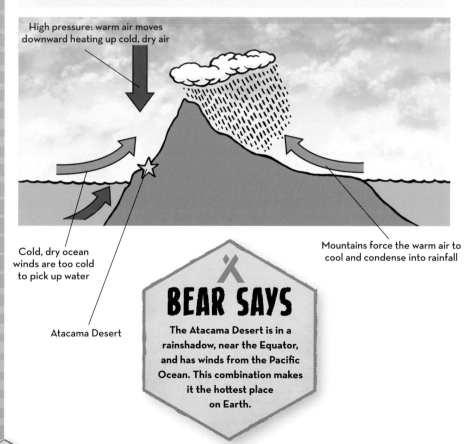

High pressure: warm air moves downward heating up cold, dry air

Cold, dry ocean winds are too cold to pick up water

Atacama Desert

Mountains force the warm air to cool and condense into rainfall

BEAR SAYS
The Atacama Desert is in a rainshadow, near the Equator, and has winds from the Pacific Ocean. This combination makes it the hottest place on Earth.

MIRAGES

Exhausted desert travellers sometimes think they can see a lake in the distance. When they arrive – the lake isn't there! This common vision in the desert is called a mirage.

What is a mirage?

A mirage is upside-down image of the bright blue sky. It is caused by the refraction (bending) of light rays travelling through the air at different temperatures. The air near the ground is hotter than air higher up in the sky, causing the refraction on the desert surface. It is not a hallucination – it often looks like there is a pool of water on the ground. The image may be shimmering because there is some movement and mixing of hot and cool air.

BEAR SAYS

Mirages are natural phenomenons that can occur both during the day and at night.

EQUIPMENT

Strong sun and very little available water are the first things to consider when packing for a desert trip. Bringing materials to make shade and carrying water are essential. It is important to consider that equipment needs protecting from sand and that it can get quite chilly during the night. Remember: finding shelter and anchoring materials can be challenging in a sandy environment.

Face mask

Food

Compass

Goggles

Space blanket

First aid kit

Shovel

BEAR SAYS

Always go with an experienced guide and make sure you have enough food and water for the time you expect to be out – plus some extra for emergencies.

Portable GPS device

Water bottle

Desert hat

Extra socks

Sleeping bag

Desert boots

UV sunglasses

A change of clothes

Sunscreen

Pen knife

Torch

Mirror

Map

Warm clothes

Parachute cord

Loose trousers

CLOTHING

Loose-fitting cotton clothing is often a good choice for desert travel. Layers of clothing will stop sweat evaporating too quickly and help prevent overheating and dehydration. Long-sleeved clothing will keep your skin covered and will protect you from sunburn and spiny plants. Desert footwear needs to keep your feet comfortable and protected from snakes and other biting animals.

Skin exposure

It is important to dress appropriately for your environment. Deserts are often very hot, but can also be extremely cold. The sun exposure in desert regions is often stronger than you are used to – you can reduce the risk of over exposure by keeping your skin covered.

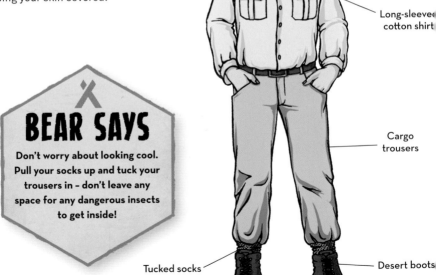

Desert hat with wind strap

Long-sleeved cotton shirt

Cargo trousers

Tucked socks

Desert boots

BEAR SAYS

Don't worry about looking cool. Pull your socks up and tuck your trousers in – don't leave any space for any dangerous insects to get inside!

COLOUR IN HOT CLIMATES

It is often thought that white is a good colour for hot climates, yet people who live in desert conditions usually wear dark colours. There are perks to wearing darker clothing – wearing a dark shirt will make you easier to spot in a desert landscape if you get lost.

Which colour would you choose?

White

White reflects heat. White clothing will reflect heat coming from your skin back towards your body. UV (Ultraviolet) light from the sun penetrates white clothing more than dark colours. UV light is harmless in small amounts, but too much can harm your skin.

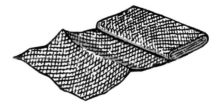

Tuareg tribesman in traditional clothing

Black

The Tuareg people have centuries of experience living in hot deserts. Their experiences have taught them that black is an excellent colour to wear in some desert conditions. Black clothing will absorb the heat from your body instead of reflecting it. If there is a breeze, loose black clothing might be a good option – the warm air around your body will be pushed out and replaced by cool air.

DESERT PLANTS

It is often thought that plants cannot grow in a desert environment – this isn't true. There are actually many different plants that can survive with small amounts of water and extremely sandy soil. These desert plants are called xerophytes. Desert plants have adapted to survive in their environments – small changes like the size of plant leaves can help stop valuable water evaporating.

Dune grass

Growing crops in the desert can be very difficult, as sand is constantly moving and covering everything with tall sand dunes. To successfully farm in the desert, the dunes need to be fixed in place. By growing dune grasses with long roots, the dunes are held in place.

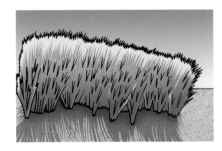

Saguaro cactus

This cactus is like a tree – it can grow over 20 m tall and can live for over 150 years. Native to Arizona, it survives hot weather and droughts by storing water – it visibly expands after rain. The fruits are edible but you would need a very long pole to get them. These plants are protected by law in Arizona so they must not be damaged.

Elephant tree

The elephant tree has adapted specifically to the hot climates of deserts in the United States. Its leaves are small – only an inch long and very narrow. It has become so good at surviving the hot weather that it has become extremely vulnerable to the cold.

Living stone

These plants get their name from their stone-like appearance. They can survive blazing hot deserts by partially burying themselves underground. In times of drought the plant can bury itself further until it is completely covered, allowing it to survive even the most extreme conditions.

Desert marigold

This is found in parts of the U.S. and Mexico. They have very hairy leaves that are essential for their survival. These leaves are important because they increase the amount of light reflected, which then lowers the leaf temperature and blocks harmful UV light. These flowers are extremely poisonous and have killed many sheep.

Mesquite tree

Mesquite trees produce beans in a pod. The pod and beans are edible and are a rich source of protein and fibres for local wildlife. Mesquite wood is highly sought after and was used in the past for ship building. It is now used to build high-quality furniture and it is expensive to buy the timber.

Ghost flower

Unlike most plants, the ghost flower does not get its energy from sunlight but feeds off fungi. This is a very unusual and rare type of plant species called myco-heterotroph. It is sometimes completely white and can also grow in very dark environments. It often flowers a few days after rainfall and only has one flower per stem.

Saltbush

The leaf surface of this plant is covered in tiny hairs that deposit salt out of the plant. This shields the plant from light, helping to keep it cool. It is found in Arizona and California, in the U.S.

Fairy duster

Commonly known as fairy duster and mock mesquite, this plant is another member of the pea family. Its seeds look like dried pea pods and are eaten by desert animals. It can flower all year round.

Old man cactus

This cactus is covered thickly with soft, white hairs that give the cactus its name. Like the desert marigold, the hairs help reflect light and lower temperature in order to survive the hot desert climate.

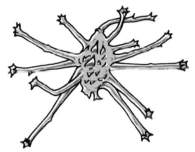

Devil's claw

Devil's claw is named after its unusually shaped fruit and is closely related to the sesame family. It is found in South Africa and is used in herbal medicine as pain relief. These plants have long, hooked seed pods that attach to moving animals. When the animal moves, the seeds are dispersed.

Prickly pear cactus

The prickly pear cactus has a spongy texture and can store water in its pods to use when there is a drought. They have thorns that stop some (but not all) animals eating them for the moisture.

BEAR SAYS

Desert plants often have features that help to collect and store water or prevent water loss.

DESERT ANIMALS

Harsh desert conditions have forced the animals that live there to adapt to the environment. Deserts have extreme temperatures and little to no water. Wildlife that have made their homes in deserts have evolved and developed natural survival tools and instincts to keep them cool and hydrated.

Camels

Most of the camels in the world are dromedary camels with one hump. Only six percent of camels have two humps. Many believe that camels store water in their humps. This is a common myth – the hump actually stores the camels' fat. By storing fat in the hump instead of around their bodies, camels are able to stay cool in the heat. Camels don't even need to drink water if there is none available, instead getting their water from green plants.

Hump for
fat storage

Thick eyelashes to
protect eyes from sand

BEAR SAYS

A thirsty camel can drink
200 litres of water in around
three minutes!

Cream coloured courser bird

These birds hunt insects by running on the ground. They lay eggs in a simple nest on the ground. Their cream colour is a natural camouflage against predators. They are classed as waders, which is unusual considering their habitat is desert.

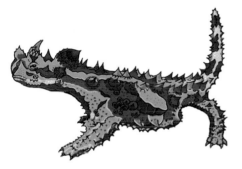

Thorny devil

This lizard has special skin that can gather all the water it needs directly from rain, standing water, and soil moisture. Its skin has a special ability to absorb water it comes into contact with, and it has scales that channel water to the corners of its mouth.

African pyxie frog

It used to be thought that these frogs died off in the dry season, but scientists have discovered that they actually bury themselves and create a cocoon that hardens around their body. They can hibernate in this cocoon for up to seven years, and when it rains the moisture makes the cocoon soften and the frog wakes up.

Kangaroo rat

Also known as the desert rat, they can survive without ever drinking water. They can jump up to 2.75 m to escape predators.

Oryx

These large antelopes feed early in the morning and late afternoon when desert temperatures are low. Oryx have an amazing ability – they can regulate their body temperature to stop sweating. By doing this they can preserve a lot of valuable water.

Fennec fox

These small foxes have very special ears – they can radiate heat and help keep their bodies cool. The ears contain lots of blood vessels that allow them to keep their blood cool, and are excellent at listening for nearby insects. Additionally, these foxes have padded feet that protect them from the hot sand.

BEAR SAYS

Some animals are dangerous, and some are edible. It is important to find information about the animals in the area you are visiting before you go.

Sidewinder rattlesnake

These snakes are named after the track they leave in the sand when they move. They are also known as the horned rattlesnake as they have little bumps that look like horns above their eyes. They are venomous, but produce a weaker venom than lots of other rattlesnakes. However, they still give a serious bite which should be treated urgently.

Desert scorpion

Desert scorpions can live in sand dunes and have extra fat to help them survive. They are nocturnal and can be found under rocks, so take care when moving rocks, in case there's a desert scorpion waiting beneath one.

Cape ground squirrel

This animal is found in southern Africa and has a bushy tail that it uses as portable shade from the desert sun. They hardly ever drink water – they can get all the water they need from the plants they eat.

Peccary

The peccary has a really tough mouth and can eat cacti without feeling the spines. This is really useful as cacti provide water as well as food.

DESERT PEOPLE

With deserts covering around a third of the Earth's surface, it is probably not surprisingly that 300 million people live there.

Tubu tribeswomen

These ladies trek for days with their camels across the Sahara desert in order to buy salt and dates. They know the location of wells on the way for water – if they make a mistake and get lost they could die.

BEAR SAYS

Living in the desert means that finding water is a high priority for most people.

Tubu tribeswoman

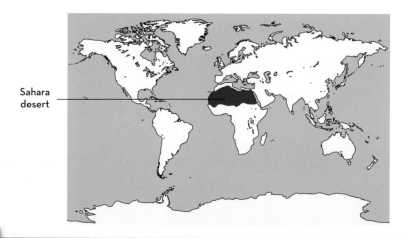

Sahara desert

Hamar people

The Hamar people are a community from southwestern Ethiopia. They are a farming community, and cattle are very important in their culture. Traditionally, boys are only considered men once they have run back and forth over the backs of their cattle.

Bedouin people

These are the best-known desert inhabitants. They often work with goats and camels – they consider camels "a gift from God" as they are so useful in every aspect of their lives. While many Bedouin have abandoned their traditional nomadic lifestyles, some still live in the desert and continue their ancient traditions of telling poetry and camel racing during celebrations.

Wodaabe beauty contests

It is hard to meet a suitable partner if you spend most of your life searching the desert for cattle pastures with your family. Every year, the Wodaabe people hold a week-long beauty contest, known as the Guérewol, where the men try to impress the ladies. Young men dress in elaborate traditional dress and face paint, and try to impress the women with songs and dances. The gathering place changes most years.

DESERT CITIES

With almost 300 million people living in deserts around the world, it is unsurprising that many large cities have developed. But how can these cities survive with so little rainfall and the constant struggle for food?

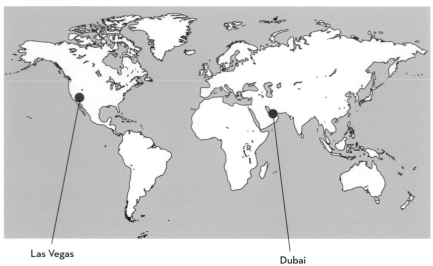

Las Vegas

Dubai

Dubai

Dubai is an oasis in a desert – on a very large scale! The oasis naturally drew crowds for the fresh water and local wildlife. It has had many functions over the years. Originally an important port for trade, oil was later discovered here in 1966 and brought wealth to the area. It was used as a refuelling base during the Gulf War. It is now widely known for its tourism, skyscrapers, and sporting events. Its hotel rooms are some of the most expensive in the world.

Las Vegas

Las Vegas is Spanish for "the meadows". It was originally a place where desert travellers could get fresh spring water, and wild grasses grew there because of the source of water. It is a desert basin, surrounded on all sides by mountain ranges. It can experience flash floods, and the drainage systems have been carefully built to cope with lots of water. This is one of the fastest growing cities in the U.S. and uses more water per person than any other city in the world. All of this in a desert! It is known for its casinos, entertainment, and nightlife.

BEAR SAYS

California has suffered from 22 years of drought over the past 100 years, with one drought lasting 7 years!

WATER

Deserts are areas with very little rain, so living conditions can be difficult for plants and animals. Water is more important than food in a survival situation. In the desert, where water is scarce, staying hydrated is a major safety concern. Humans can live for weeks without food, but without water you can die in a few days – even in fairly cool conditions.

Why is water important?

The human body is about 60 percent water. It keeps us the correct temperature, moves substances around our bodies, and helps to get rid of waste. We cannot live for more than about 3–5 days without water.

BEAR SAYS

In the desert you should drink at least one gallon per day, and drink before you get thirsty. If your pee is almost clear then you are properly hydrated.

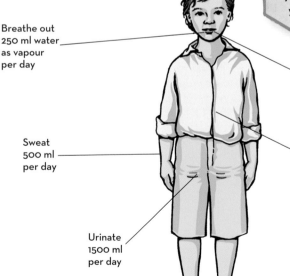

Breathe out 250 ml water as vapour per day

Usually drink 2 L per day

Sweat 500 ml per day

250 ml comes from food

Urinate 1500 ml per day

Oasis

An oasis is an isolated place in a desert where there is water, and plants grow. Animals and humans often make habitats at an oasis if it is large enough to support the group. The water is from an underground river reaching the surface and forming a spring, pond, or lake. An oasis is a very important place for people and animals in a desert, and if a particular tribe has control of an oasis then they can control the trade in that area.

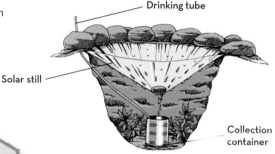

Drinking tube

Solar still

Collection container

Solar still

A solar still is a process used to gather moisture from plants to make drinking water. A hole is dug and some plants are placed in the hole – they can be planted if it is going to be used for a while. Moisture evaporates from the plants, rises and condenses on the underside of a plastic sheet, then drips into a collection container. It can be drunk without disturbing the system by using a drinking tube.

BEAR SAYS

If you see bees, flies, mosquitoes, or frogs you are likely to be less than 3 miles from water.

Water from cuttings

Place as many plant cuttings as possible in a bag – just make sure they don't touch the sides. Prop up the centre of the bag to form a tent shape. Put the bag on a slope so that the water can run to a corner to make collection easy.

NAVIGATION

Deserts are difficult to navigate as there are very few permanent landmarks and the sand dunes are constantly changing and moving, making them unreliable navigation points. Distance can be difficult to judge, and sandstorms can make visibility difficult or even impossible. Getting lost is a very dangerous risk as water and food can be a long way away, and travelling at any speed can be difficult due to the heat and the lack of proper road surfaces.

Navigating using shadows

During the day you can always use the sun to determine direction. The sun will always rise in the east and settle in the west. This means your shadow points west in the morning, north in the afternoon, and east in the evenings. You can use these rules to help you navigate in the wild when you do not have your compass.

BEAR SAYS

Always go with an experienced guide, take a map, a GPS system, and more food and water than you need.

GPS

This device can receive information from special satellites in space and accurately calculate its geographical location. It may have a poor signal in urban areas but is ideal when travelling. Make sure to always check your GPS is working where you travel and that you have enough batteries for the duration of your trip, plus some spares.

Navigating using stars

Stars have been used for navigation for centuries. By knowing your constellations, you can navigate on starry nights. In the Northern Hemisphere the constellation Ursa Minor (the plough) can usually be easily found. The constellation appears to rotate through the sky at night, but this is because of the rotation of Earth. The plough has two "pointer stars" that always point to the North Star, a star that is always to the north.

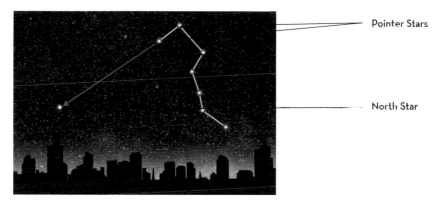

Pointer Stars

North Star

Southern Crux

In the Southern Hemisphere the stars appear to rotate in a clockwise direction, and the constellation Crux is used for navigation. It is four bright stars in a kite shape and the furthest star indicates the direction of the South pole – but beware – there is also a group of stars known as the "false cross".

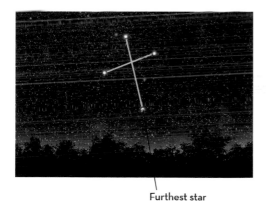

Furthest star

BEAR SAYS

It has been reported that blind nomads navigate in the desert using their sense of smell!

SHELTER

If you are lost in the desert, the best way to survive is to build a shelter and wait for help to arrive. You will lose less water from your body in the shade and keep warmer at night. Be careful not to disturb scorpions and snakes if you are digging – always use a shovel or a stick and spend time planning your shelter before you start so you don't waste effort on something unsuitable or in the wrong location.

Below-ground shelter

In some situations a shelter underground may be your best option. It can protect you from heat as well as cold and attacks or extreme weather. However, this needs to be balanced by the fact that the shelter will take more effort to build than one above ground. If it is very hot it might need to be done at night. The double cover is very useful to keep the temperature down if you have enough material.

Open desert shelter

This might be useful to take advantage of any breeze, again the double layer will help keep temperatures down. Make sure it is secure for windy conditions.

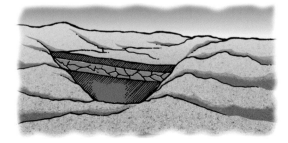

STAYING WELL IN THE DESERT

Basic first aid knowledge is an essential part of survival. There are lots of places you can learn some basic skills – in a couple of hours you can learn and practise techniques that could save a life. When going on an adventure you should make sure you have a first aid kit, and that you plan for the environment you are expecting. A desert first aid kit should always contain equipment to deal with sunburn, dehydration, and insect bites.

Heat exhaustion

This is when a person becomes very hot and starts to lose water or salt. If they don't get treatment they are at risk of heatstroke. Some of the symptoms of heat exhaustion are:

- Tiredness and weakness
- Feeling dizzy and faint
- Lower blood pressure
- Headache
- Muscle cramps
- Sickness
- Heavy sweating
- Extreme thirst
- A fast pulse
- Urinating less often, dark coloured urine

Treatment for heat exhaustion

When someone has heat exhaustion they need to lie down in the shade. Remove as much clothing as possible, cool their skin with water (you could wrap them in a wet sheet), fan their wet skin, and give them plenty of water, diluted squash, or a sports drink. If they don't start to get better within 30 minutes, call for medical help.

Heatstroke

This is very serious but not as common as heat exhaustion. It occurs when a person's temperature becomes very high and their body cannot cool down without help. It can be fatal, so a person with heatstroke needs urgent medical attention.

Dehydration

Dehydration is when someone loses more fluid through sweating, vomiting, diarrhoea, or urinating than they have taken in from eating and drinking. It is important for everyone to drink plenty but especially if they are exercising more than normal, are in a hot place, have a fever, have diarrhoea or vomiting, or are elderly or very young.

Treatment for dehydration

You should treat dehydration by drinking plenty of water, taking a suitable oral rehydration solution (you can buy this in sachets from a chemist), resting, and massaging cramped muscles. If the person doesn't get better fast – get them to a doctor.

BEAR SAYS

The signs of dehydration include headache, dry mouth, small amounts of dark urine, and muscle cramps.

Rehydration solution

Sunburn

If a person shows any signs of sunburn, get them to move to the shade, or preferably indoors. Take a cool bath or shower, apply aftersun lotion, and ask an adult to give them a suitable painkiller if they need it. After being out in the sun, you are at risk of dehydration so it is important to drink plenty of water and keep an eye out for signs of heat exhaustion or heatstroke.

BEAR SAYS

Sunburn is usually preventable by making sure you stay out of the sun, cover up, and wear sunscreen. Planning is key.

Scorpion

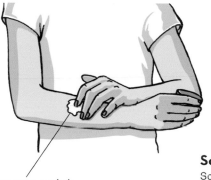

Suncream can help prevent sunburn

Scorpion sting

Scorpion stings can vary a lot. Most will cause slight pain and swelling, but about 25 out of around 1500 species can cause serious harm to a healthy adult. It is always worth keeping an eye out for an allergic reaction to any scorpion sting.

BEAR SAYS

Take care when lifting rocks and shake out clothing and boots to check for scorpions before you get dressed.

Treating scorpion stings

If someone is stung by a scorpion, always call for medical assistance, describing the scorpion if at all possible.

- Keep the victim calm.
- Wash and dry stung area.
- Use ice to keep swelling down.
- Keep stung area below heart level to slow down the spread of venom.
- Ask an adult for a suitable painkiller.
- If the person stops breathing follow first aid procedures, performing CPR and rescue breaths if necessary.

FINDING FOOD IN THE DESERT

When travelling in the desert it is important to consider how much food to take and how you would survive if you got lost. Fresh food will go bad quickly in hot conditions and you may not want heavy tins if you have to carry everything yourself. While you can sometimes find edible plants and animals, it is worth learning how to identify safe foods to eat before you travel so that you can find food in an emergency situation.

Tuareg survival

A Tuareg nomadic person from the Sahara desert claims that you can survive for nine days on just three dates. We don't recommend you try this!

Day 1 – eat a date skin
Day 2 – eat a date skin
Day 3 – eat a date skin
Day 4 – eat the flesh of one date
Day 5 - eat the flesh of one date
Day 6 – eat the flesh of one date
Day 7 – suck on one date stone
Day 8 – suck on one date stone
Day 9 – suck on one date stone
Day 10 – you will die unless you get a drink today!

Be careful

While humans can usually survive for about three weeks without food, it is vital to eat properly if at all possible to have the energy to move around – especially important if you are travelling in harsh conditions. It is important to take care not to eat anything poisonous if you run out of food. Only eat what you can identify and know to be safe.

Date tree

Top tips for finding food

1. If water is not available, do not eat, as the food will increase your need for water. Don't waste energy looking for food unless you already have water.
2. Avoid plants with milky sap, red beans, anything that tastes bitter or soapy, spines, fine hairs or thorns, anything with dill, carrot, parsnip or parsley-like leaves, anything that smells of almonds, anything with three leaves.
3. Boil plants if possible.
4. Use the "universal edibility test" (page 36).
5. Trapping is easier than hunting.

BEAR SAYS

All cactus fruit are safe to eat – however, getting to them can be dangerous and painful!

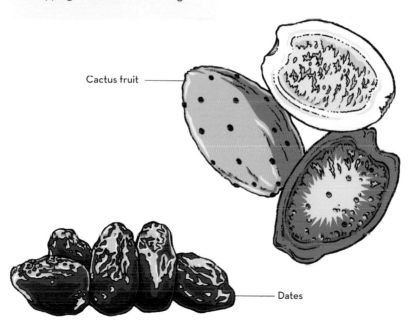

Cactus fruit

Dates

Universal edibility test

1. Don't eat for eight hours. During this time, place a piece of the plant on the inside of your wrist for 15 minutes to see if you have a reaction.
2. Only test one part of the plant at a time. Some plants have parts that are edible and other parts that are poisonous.
3. Smell the food. Check for strong or acidic smells.
4. Only drink purified water.
5. Touch a pinch of the food to your outer lip and wait for three minutes to see if there is any burning or itching.
6. If there is no reaction, place the same piece on your tongue and hold it there for 15 minutes.
7. If there is no reaction, chew it and hold it in your mouth for 15 minutes – do not swallow!
8. If no reaction occurs, swallow it.
9. Wait eight hours. If there is no reaction, eat a slightly bigger portion of the same part prepared in the same way.
10. Wait another eight hours. If there is still no reaction this part of the plant prepared in this way is safe to eat.

BEAR SAYS

Boiling water will purify it so that it is safe to drink.

BEAR SAYS

Never eat anything you do not know about – some plants can kill! Only use the universal edibility test as a last resort if you have no alternative.

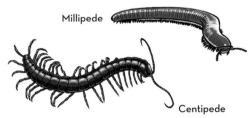

Millipede

Centipede

Be careful

Lots of things we wouldn't usually consider eating are actually a good source of nutrition. Scorpions are edible apart from their venomous tails. Centipedes are edible, but be careful – millipedes are very similar but are poisonous.

DESERT SURVIVAL STORIES

The desert can be a very uncomfortable place to be unless you have the correct equipment, supplies, and knowledge. People are few and far between, so often help isn't nearby. Travelling is tricky because of the heat, and finding water can be extremely difficult, so people often don't survive for very long without proper planning.

Marathon de Sables

In 1994 a man called Mauro Prosperi was running the famous Marathon des Sables race, and he encountered a sandstorm just after the start. He got confused and when the storm stopped he ended up running in the wrong direction. When he realised he was lost, he urinated into a bottle and made the liquid last three days. He walked early in the morning and in the evening, and took shelter in the middle of the day. Eventually he found a shrine and drank the blood from some bats that he caught. He walked for a further five days and eventually came to an oasis where some nomads found him and took him to safety.

BEAR SAYS

Prosperi entered the race again four years later but still didn't finish because he stubbed his toe! But we love his courageous spirit.

James Riley

James Riley was a nineteenth-century sea captain. His ship ran aground off the Moroccan coast of the Sahara desert and there was only salted pork to eat and no water for him and his crew. They were found by local people who took them into slavery. They were marched through the desert and forced to drink camel urine to survive. Riley told their captors that there was a rich person in one of the towns who would pay to release them. He wrote a note to the French, English, and Spanish consuls and begged them to find someone to buy him and his men. Luckily, the English consul got the note and agreed a price for their release.

Walking to Arizona

A young man needed to get from Utah to Arizona. He decided to walk there with his dog – about 90 miles through unforgiving desert. His dog ran off, he ran out of food, and left behind his heavy bag, but luckily followed a river. After about two weeks he was reported missing. The local sheriff sent a helicopter to fly along the length of the river. After three weeks in the desert he was found. His rescuers thought that if he had been out for another 24 hours he would have likely died.

The tragedy at Kufra

In 1942, 12 members of the South African air force were sent in three planes to an oasis at Kufra in the Libyan desert. There were some problems with the weather forecast and some misheard radio communications. After one of the aircraft had some engine problems, they all landed in the desert. Following several unsuccessful short flights attempting to find help they were stuck in a sandstorm and ran out of water. These men were not trained in desert survival and had no appropriate equipment. They drank the liquid from their compasses (which was poisonous) and sprayed themselves with the fire extinguishers to cool down (the chemicals gave them painful skin injuries). All but one man died.

BEAR SAYS

As a result of this tragedy, procedures were changed so that suitable equipment is carried, and people are better trained and experienced before they fly.

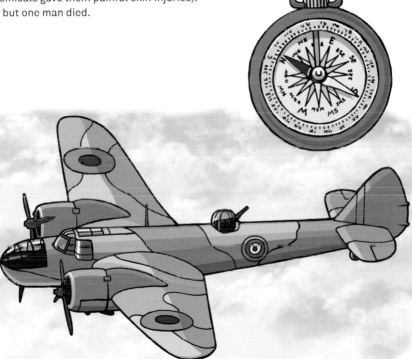

Five days in a ravine

In 2011, an elderly man got lost after leaving a restaurant in Arizona. He tried to turn his car around but slid into a ravine. He couldn't get a mobile phone signal, and fell over when he tried to get out of the car, so he stayed where he was for five days until he was found by some people out hiking.

He had been drinking windscreen washer fluid and was lucky not to die as it is poisonous. It was extremely cold at night in the desert in winter, but luckily not as hot as summer in the middle of the day.

Hitchhiking

A man called Ricky Gilmore was hitchhiking in New Mexico to a nearby town to buy some alcohol. He got a lift and the couple who picked him up asked him to share it.

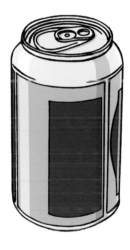

He refused and they got cross and dumped him out of the car in the middle of the desert. What made things worse was that Gilmore was a wheelchair user and his chair was back at his house. Over three days he dragged himself four miles without food or water before somebody stopped to help him. He spent more than a week in hospital recovering.

DUST AND SANDSTORMS

Sandstorms happen when wind picks up sand and carries it a long way in a cloud of dust and sand. It can be scary to be in a sandstorm – you cannot see anything and your eyes, mouth, and nose are coated in sand.

Sandstorms

Sandstorms are most common on bare, flat ground, like the Sahara desert. They happen mainly in summer in certain places in the U.S., such as Kansas and Oklahoma, where the topsoil is blown around.

Goggles and face mask will protect your eyes and face from the flying sand

In March 2014, people in the UK were surprised to wake up to find a thin layer of red dust on their cars. This dust came from the Sahara desert. Strong winds in the Sahara had lifted the dust off the ground and high into the atmosphere. The dust was transported thousands of miles to the UK, and when it rained the water drops collected dust particles on the way down. The layer of dust was left behind when the water eventually evaporated after it rained.

Sandstorm survival

- Listen to local TV or radio information for sandstorm warnings.
- Take a blanket, goggles, mask, and water with you.
- Put a mask over your nose and mouth if you have one. If you don't have a mask, put a damp cloth over your nose and mouth.
- You can put a small amount of petroleum jelly inside your nostrils to stop your nose drying out.
- Wear goggles, or shield your eyes with your arm, and then wrap a cloth around your eyes and ears.
- Find shelter as quickly as possible. If there is no shelter nearby, crouch down low and keep your mouth and eyes protected from the flying sand.
- Keep as much skin and face covered as possible.
- Get to high ground – the storm will be less forceful at the top of a hill.
- If you are with a camel, get it to sit down and press yourself against its sheltered side – camels are good at coping with sandstorms.
- Stay low to the ground and protect yourself from flying objects – wind-propelled sand hurts!
- Stay where you are until the storm passes.

Sandstorm impact

Sandstorms might be just wind and dust but they can cause a lot of damage. Electrical equipment, tools, homes, and crops are all at risk of being buried or damaged by the force of the sand. Sandstorms can move entire sand dunes and bury crops with the displaced sand. This is an issue desert tribes face every year.

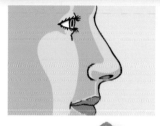

BEAR SAYS

You can often outrun a sandstorm in a car, as they travel quite slowly. If it catches up with you, stop the car, roll up the windows, close the air vents, and wait for the storm to end.

DESERT AT NIGHT

The sun can heat up the desert to extremely high temperatures during the day, but at night the desert can be a very cold place. This is because the sun's heat warms the air during the day but at night the warm air escapes upwards because there aren't any clouds to trap the heat in. The desert is an area of low humidity and this is also partly why the temperatures reached in the day are so different to temperatures at night.

Desert animals at night

Desert animals are often more active at night, hunting for food, water, or a mate! Many mammals, birds, and insects are nocturnal and the sound of them at night can be a surprise. The colder air and ground temperatures make it easier for them to move around.

BEAR SAYS

During the day, desert temperatures can go as high as 50°C, but at night it may fall to below 0°C.

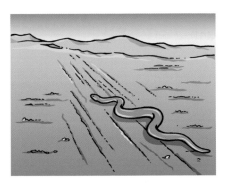

Survival at night

- Make sure you have the correct equipment, a good torch, and a warm sleeping bag.
- Travel at sunset, at night, and in the early morning. Rest during the day if at all possible.
- Light a fire to keep warm and keep animals away if you aren't moving.
- Wear lots of layers so that you can regulate your temperature.
- Watch out for nocturnal wildlife.

Thermal imaging device
This technology builds a picture using heat given off by objects. It is most useful in near-absolute darkness, or when detecting people.

Night vision goggles
These work by collecting all available light, including some that we can't see with the naked eye, and boosting it using clever electronics so that the image is clearly visible.

GLOSSARY

Arid – a land area having little or no rain.

Climate – the general weather conditions for a particular area.

Condensation – water that collects on a surface.

Consul – an official person in a foreign country that looks after people from their own country when they are visiting.

CPR – cardiopulmonary resuscitation – a life-saving procedure carried out when somebody's breathing or heart has stopped.

Drought – a long period with less than normal rainfall causing a shortage of water.

Dune – a mound or ridge of sand formed by the wind.

Evaporation – process of water turning into vapour.

Habitat – the natural environment of a living thing.

Hallucination – a person thinking they see or hear something that isn't really there.

Humidity – the amount of water vapour in the air.

Meteorologist – a scientist that studies the weather.

Moisture – a small amount of water.

Nocturnal – something that is active at night.

Northern hemisphere – the half of the Earth that is north of the Equator.

Nutrition – the process of eating the right food for health and growth.

Precipitation – water that falls to the ground as rain, sleet, or snow.

Prevailing wind – the most frequent wind direction that is experienced at a particular place.

Ravine – a deep, narrow gorge with steep sides.

Shrine – a religious building or shelter.

Southern hemisphere – the half of the Earth that is south of the Equator.

UV light – Ultraviolet light – an invisible part of the electromagnetic spectrum.

Venomous – an animal that can inject venom, usually by biting.

Discover more amazing books in the Bear Grylls series:

Perfect for young adventurers, the *Survival Skills* series accompanies an exciting range of colouring and activity books. Curious kids can also learn tips and tricks for almost any extreme situation in *Survival Camp*, explore Earth in *Extreme Planet*, and discover some of history's greatest explorers in the *Epic Adventures* series.

Conceived by Weldon Owen in partnership with Bear Grylls Ventures

Produced by Weldon Owen, an imprint of Kings Road Publishing
Suite 3.08 The Plaza, 535 Kings Road,
London SW10 0SZ, UK

WELDON OWEN
Publisher Donna Gregory
Designer Shahid Mahmood
Editor Susie Rae
Editorial Assistant Thomas McBrien
Contributor Anne Farthing
Illustrator Julian Baker
Cover image © 2018 Bear Grylls Ventures

Printed in Malaysia
2 4 6 8 10 9 7 5 3 1

Disclaimer
Weldon Owen and Bear Grylls take pride in doing our best to get the facts right in putting together the information in this book, but occasionally something slips past our beady eyes. Therefore we make no warranties about the accuracy or completeness of the information in the book and to the maximum extent permitted, we disclaim all liability. Wherever possible, we will endeavour to correct any errors of fact at reprint.

Kids – if you want to try any of the activities in this book, please ask your parents first! Parents – all outdoor activities carry some degree of risk and we recommend that anyone participating in these activities be aware of the risks involved and seek professional instruction and guidance. None of the health/medical information in this book is intended as a substitute for professional medical advice; always seek the advice of a qualified practitioner.

A WELDON OWEN PRODUCTION. AN IMPRINT OF KINGS ROAD PUBLISHING.
PART OF THE BONNIER PUBLISHING GROUP.